Mysticism

Mysticism

Jeremy Garcia

Cody Adam

Contents

Contents

Contents

{ 1 }

Contents

Age 17

Told I was forgiven
The mark of doom
Am I to change?
A sinful behavior stop by the shock of cause
Ability of no regret in being sorry
With the sensitivity of empathy flowing in the wind
Symphony is self taught for no bad choice
My thoughts wonder of my freedom
Shackle gone, forgiven
Am I to learn?
Taught the stop of bad behavior
Ability to be sorry without guilt
As the moon shines of my past
Lighten touch of thoughts to act in carefulness
Said I'm forgiven
Free from eternal damnation received from a sinful act in
regarding to brighten the chance of learn.

My Sin

I repent, time spent
Ask forgiveness from God
Release of pressure consume me from his nod
I repent, time spent
Bad habits tend to stop matured into sod
Confirmation of Creator's doing as a steel rod
I repent, time spent
Stable living healthy in the mod
Action from the invisible pod
I repent, time spent
I ask forgiveness in growth of knowing God

{ 4 }

Part of Me

Sin is part of me
I apart from it
For Godly is to be
Realize I'm weak
With having a will powered by God
The strength to refuse sin is at seek
To be complete without evil at hand
Commit to obey the lord
Be in paradise of no wickedness in stand
Sin is part of me
Yet I came to apart from it
For Godly is always to be.

His Existence

I failed, was in monstrous play in everyday
My consciousness delay knowing right from wrong in
my sway
I hailed sin from lusty clay
In the dark having no humanity in my day
Still God alerts his existence at the bay
To achieve success in righteous of knowingly may and be
in dear away from sinning in everyway
I came to his know
Forgiveness glow
Forward without sinful show
In my delight of the outcome of my sin.

Act of He

The invisible strength of he
Keeping one steady in life of the tree
Learn from mistakes, still happy in harmony
Having love ones in life is the charm of he
Making forgiveness bright taught lesson as it's the biggest
message of the age
Growing to be wise collected in paradise in the heart of
he in cleanse sage
Still he aims life to be his way,
With learning life in human govern sway
The journey of keeping one stable is the satisfaction as
seven day rested with human in love with its God.

All My Life

All my life God I heard and hear you

I best not to deny you, as I best to live in this times

Yet all I see is sin, a place after their death for to pay for their crimes

Naked men and women, Guns being the best choice for solution, force touching doesn't stop in the ones of pure sin, Crazy has it's defined in evolution, souls defining pain having to see it again

All my life God I heard and hear you

I best not deny you, for your satisfaction of life is the only way to feel about life.

As I see sin, forgiven speaks in my soul, having the glory of Jesus Christ win, as I go along with it's show, the firmness faith to have it stop, is the call of the will of God having its pop, alertness across the earth. Where eyes and ears that sense he has its faithful girth

All my life I have heard and hear you God.

My Belief in God

My mind is clear being held by God
His sight is near, being meld into God
No reason to fear, being weld to God
Heaven is here, Agreeing, yelled from God.
I make faith from my belief in God to vanish sin in life
I awake faith from my belief in God to banish sin in life.

{ 9 }

Bless Me

Bless me once, bless me twice, and bless me again
My natural heart aim to not sin
Love to be a dear to a soul in the path of life as a friendly animal
Shine positivity to direct no sin
Be in faith for tomorrow in having no wrong doing, giving a healthy band a ball,
To appear the hero in God, correct thinking without sin
Being a fisherman in land a haul
Being plentiful in wealth of proper is what I desire
No wrong doing for hire
Bless me once, bless me twice, and bless me again
I clear path to God in just existence by obeying the commandments
Having the will to confess my sin and move in betterness delight of he
I'm your worshipper in matured light in forgiveness

JEREMY GARCIA

In the world having a second chance, spending it away from sin in the mystic from God to be

Having a comfort in living with darkness where God only gives light

I'm the one that prays for neighbors in tender might to have no plea

Be perfect in God eyes in harmony, be sane in the right arm of he

So, bless me once, bless me twice, and bless me again.

{ **10** }

Bless Me Well God

Bless me well, care for me dear
Bless me God, heal my tear
Know my will to end sin is near
Tender my soul into your gear
Bless me well, for the gift I've seen
Bless me God as I direct you to them in between
Know my will grows the land filled with green
Tender my soul in direction of your scene
Bless me, have me be in your care
Bless me God, for my love is fair
Know my will to be without sin is paying the fare
Tender my soul into the arms of you to bare
Bless me well God from my will to be Godly.

{ **11** }

Thinking

Comfy mood
Eyes closed
Moon jeweled
Deep relaxation exposed
That I know Creator keeps me at bay
He always standby to safeguard my way
Comfy mood
Eyes closed
Not in rude
Calmness dispose
That I know Creator keeps me assured
Having the natural existence of him insured
Comfy mood, eyes closed in paradise by positive thinking
of a God.

{ **12** }

Horizon to Meet

The horizon to meet in thanks to Creator
As the king with the earth, once eat her
Told her you will be a new earth
All humans will be more than angels as one girth
The day of the king, shall it be here in no time
I say of the king, life without father is the greatest crime
Centuries of sin caress the King's words
Alive the end of sin caress what the king has heard
Be in the air to meet his return
Reality it be, all humans has the need of the next to yearn
The king Jesus Christ is the one to do this of our will to belief in the only father
The king Jesus Christ is the one to will us to be in the belief in the only father.

Still Will

She wears a mask that she has found
Comes a husband with heart of love, pound for pound
And I know her behind the mask
Loves to be alone and sex with richness at times
Being free to succeed any task
Yet her thoughts being paired to one chimes
She gets married and paints her freedom
Each color is a male of her dreams
Kisses her husband in memory scenes to see them
Her aloneness shows in her painting's with colorful beams
Distant became between us for being as one with a love
one is the standard in life.

Choice of Faith

I see my choice, within the darkness noise
Hearing God's voice, giving me direction of poise
Still the devil is on my trail
Handshake broken by God and it wail
Screams, I have given you my time, rejection is a crime!
Steadfast having faith in God winning the war
Obeying doing no harm godly gore
My choice is the Christian God to miracle lives evermore.

{ 15 }

To Be Real

I heart you not to be in sin in the city, not to be ungodly in the country, with finding the love to fit me, in the will of the lord to have love hump me, to the paradise of sharing a life with one, kiss to be in bliss where positivity has won my mark to be real

I faith you in having direction away from sin as loud as a rock n roll concert in the city, not to be in a path of evil as hard beat as a hip hop concert in the country, with finding the love to hit me, as loud to crump me, with joy in sharing life with one, hug in snug positivity has won my mark to be real

I love you and not met you in sin of the city, not being a evil doers of the country, in finding the love to get me, in the will and grace of God to have the holy spirit thump me. With ability to miracle as sharing life with one, caress in impress positivity that won my mark to be real

Honestly, have no darkness, in the chance to be real.

My God

Bless me by believing in you
You are truth, true so true
Bless me by my love for you
Where there is no blue, no deep blue
Bless me by my faith in you
Obeying the rules doing the do, Harmless do
Bless me by my walk for you
Loving and forgiving the enemy while not sinning too
Bless me by my life in talk with you
Make all negative go away, make it shoo
Bless me my God in Jesus Christ, amen.

Aware To Be

Aware to be
Someone with hope of a Creator
With acts in meaning of the existence of the supreme
being
Alive now and later
In life with no sin is seeing
Aware to be
The one having a custom road with the Creator
With scenes meaning of wealth in caring from the su-
preme being
Always alive now with faith alive later
In the know not to sin in everyday seeing
Aware to be
Being as one with the Creator
In note to be fully in conscious of life in the supreme being
Lively alive now to lively be later
The form in having strength to resist sin to be in holi-
ness seeing

Mysticism

Aware to be, in care of he.

The Gift

Being held in his tender heart, markings from sin not being tart

Shocking from his existence from the start, by keeping me well lived in the story of art

Being caressed by his tender love, having the ability to grow as a clove

In the habitat he made by us of, with the direction to living paradise in structure he naturally hove

Thanking the witnesses of he to live the word in we, in shine of awakening in betterness sense of living life in the world so free

Ability to be Christian is the best gift from this earth.

{ **19** }

My Faith

Children dead by gun fire
Sickness captures souls without for hire
Forceful touching, hard to trust this
Cold cases long for justice
What's the frequency Jesus Christ?
As of days of Noah, worst to be without father
Has the ways of Noah, burst to be within father
Having faith over the years, for the direction of sin has no way in being found
Having faith with the shone tears, for the direction of sin has no way in being sound
The ability to be drunken without the darkness grin, is my faith to be without sin.

I Faith

Well, I faith, miracle
Yes I do, glory to the lord
Have it shine, have it run free, on its grind, to complete be
In the wonder of natural mystic caring for neighbor
In the thunder of factual mystic baring for neighbor
I have faith for miracle to one in dearest need of the
lord's actual
In will saithe the lord for miracle to one in nearest need
of the lord's factual
I faith miracle, Yes I do
It has it fun, heartful to the broken dew
Give the ability to put down the gun, to be with just one
not a few,
In steady love from God, so true
In obeying the law of God to do.

{ **21** }

Faith

Be faithful while living life among sin
Desire to be with God more alone
Enjoying the element of praying
Having the consciousness to witness the king on his throne
Swaying with the mass that is right from having sin
Loving he with soul, in life bone
Four hearts were tender gift from God
One for each wind, may have no sin to shone
Forgiven to try in the one whole being
Yet my muse whom I phone
The gift from God to be godly
I'm the base, and Jesus Christ is the top of the cone
In faith of a God to shed light to the dark
Praying to he to give light it's tone
Being the existence with the supreme in just
Having only my faith to own
In relation with a God all knowing of his ability in my
earthy home.

You Faith Me To Be

You faith me, give me sense of power
Direction without sin is the hour
Breeze of no harm, no acts of sour
The ability to be in heaven, no enemy devour
Honestly being in the sight of he
Happily being in the right of he
Is the presence of you in the life in the tree
You faith me ever so be
To be a part of Jesus Christ the king and our father God.

{ **23** }

Faithful Walk

As the preacher mates with own lover in godly manner, I wrestle with the devil with sinners of the city, having a friendly spoken banner,

I await for a lover while I work to delight God to be alive, to message of no sinful acts in my walk on their moonlight drive,

Penetrating the elders in their graves as a shaman to shed miracles among the earth, beating American tom-tom in belief of Jesus Christ's girth,

Every pound makes faithful sound

While the children are dead, not alive, I awake the elders as a native American dancing on their graves by my faith to miracle's God said in my walk on their moonlight drive

I say I love you dearly, no reason the elders to fear me,

I know my faith act will message the lord, send an angel with a mighty sword,

to stop the sinning, where bad guys turn to be in the winning among my walk in their moonlight drive.

{ 24 }

He Stares At Her

Delightful Hand
Being with me, understand
The best comfort having a partner
Going together like seasons
Mating, romancing the time
Having to look no further
Having all the reasons
To be the best half to the rhyme
My delightful wife's hand, the day I took the oath, my stand.

{ 25 }

Faith in Death

Rest everything will be okay
God will do his love for us
Rest everything will be more array
God will direct his love with us
Have faith, the belief of passion
Hath saithe, the relief of compassion
Forgiveness opens the door of heaven where the father
is at hand
   Recognizing the mystic of the natural touch of God in
grand
   Gives the invisible works the will in earth
   As is in heaven is in earth
   Rest everything is be done in harmony for us by the in-
visible God over us all.

{ **26** }

Spiritual

She becomes alive in my dreams
Act of God showing her in glowing beams
We kiss, act in love knowing we together, no need to miss
She reacts in reality of sanity rested love
The complete notion on how to connect to her from above
Is god's delight smiling as a clown
Glorifying his ability in true love from her frown
Alive, the movie star
No jive, belief in God to go far
In my hearty hive
Is to be with me she says at the bar
In joint communion by afar
God gives us the ability to connect
Mystic founding in being correct
In wonders of love intellect
By the power of God seeing us through
She becomes alive in my dreams making mystic true.

{ 27 }

Faithful

Seat me there
Faithful to miracle a care
Greet me there
Faithful in miracles to bare
Meet he there
Faithful for miracles to wear
Tweet he there
Faithful so human and miracle to pair.

{ 28 }

Insight

In the dark with the devil, I offend
Close my bark with the devil, I attend
God
Given a second chance with my senses, I'm corrected to
Being in the light from my pre tenses, I'm directed to
God
Thankful in knowing my head on straight
Thankful in glowing my life in straight.

Away From Sin

I'm finally away from sin. I can breathe
Prioritize my path with the lord, to can weave
My life in his reality to succeed in humanity's path
To be in better enlightenment away from the lord's wrath
I'm away from sin able to think
Stories to amuse the lord to blink
In clearer sight to live without dark
Able to function as knowing why all dogs has a bark
Yes im being without sin, closer to God from the channel
in my soul
No will to do fleshy, only spiritual acts complete, I'm
be whole
In faith of miracles as it's a miracle that I'm clear for-
given, having a chance
The direction of no sin, no desire to will my activities in
sin, only now God's grace to enhance
Away from sin, my soul can be alive more
Away from sin, my soul close to God to adore.

{ **30** }

Disciple pt. one

I pray for myself and all neighbor
Struggles seem to end, and needs amend
Day in the sun without harm from the heat saber
No sin to attend, in peace mystic trend
Notice of bad behavior becomes taper
The power of prayer has no end, existing to exist God in amend
Another day being a vapor
Ending sin to bend, the natural in positivity tend
To be stable more as a skyscraper
Shine in the clear is the sight of I pray for myself and pray for all neighbor.

{ 31 }

Disciple pt. Two

Looking within
Seeing no harm
Yet darkness covered my soul
Lost complete control
Deep in sin
Lusty charm
I arose to be tame with God
Is to be a I look within
Having faith to sight miracle alive
My path in obeying with being forgiving
The presence of tender care from God as in miracle
To have it happen to all, not particle
Yes in his name it can be
Faithful looking within to give all the feel of assured by
God in the tree of life.

His Word

Read me a verse of the master,
Explode my life in holiness as time goes by faster,
Dead on the run with a second chance
Said having no gun in my pants,
Being faithful to be corrected,
Being faithful to be selected
Having prayer in strength in depths of love
Having prayer in effect from the depths from above
No will to sin
No thrill from sin
Cherishing the invisible way in mystic of God
Perishing sin from the visible say in mystic of God
Best to be away from sin in my day
Being bless in the leeway
His words is the world in my may
Read me a verse of the master,
Words being the answer with excitement going faster
Being in the everlasting in the here after

With the innocence of a baby's laughter
Redeem my soul in his words being alive
Being in sanity thinking with my art no being jive
The caress of believing to become real tenders life on
earth with his word
Being not involve is absolutely absurd
The light of living in his sentences
Is free rent in his
With obeying the commandments in return
I glow of another to know God in my days of yearn
Life in sanity is verses of the master, I believe in God in
the earth while sin blast her.

{ **33** }

Whats Going On?

Whole lot of bleeding going on

The highly developed are in peace while the madman rapes and kills in the time of talk of war

The healing is in the thoughts and actions to partake in no harming manner with wise decisions to stabilize life in the habitat given

Whole lot of sickness living on

The highly developed are in peace while the madwoman in mental distress steals and kills in the time of walk of war

The healing is the notion and motion in positive manner at all the time living life in the habitat given

The hero keeps faith in father to astray, wrongdoing one day, while a king is being prepared to return in life's sway.

Deeply in the Thought
of She

Thinking of you deeply
The fairytale we live shapes me
In God matured to have your kiss
Passion of continuous bliss in meeting you in swiss, con-
nection with God
Not a ghost you are, but more than an angel
Thinking of you deeply
As God has you be more mystical than your fleshy life
here on earth.

Thumpin and Bumpin

Bumpin Christ in my soul
Thumpin Christ on the devil's know
Being in clarity of life, paradise here without a wife
Best to obey he, Bless in complete me
Miracle wishing, Faith of it blissing
Sight fishing, Prayer not missing
God the closeness of you, be there as you dew
God the hostness of you, Be there as you do
Light shining in the dark
Might grinding from its bark
Miracle is the word
It's define is all I heard
Praying for it
Give reasons to store it
Make the devil powerless and lose
Make sin fry and have it not choose
In the world my king, you are alive in every boy and girl
Forgive me to best miracle the life in the swirl

JEREMY GARCIA

Thumpin Christ, on the devil's know
Bumpin Christ in my soul.

Steady Praying

Steady praying everyday for health, wealth and be stable living this life

Had experience with she enough to dwell alone having father to be my wife

The path in being tender is well in the hellos friendly to lead somewhere

Is the force of God in assured politeness in exchange to heed some care

Having this experience happen completes my prayer in being safe in the times of sin

Health and wealth to play along, stable enough to repeat again

Is the power from God in my life to achieve his glory loud to succeed righteous

My faith only Creator can bright this

To be insured in living life rightful

To the end of flesh to be in the light whole

Steady praying for health, wealth and be stable to live this life.

{ 37 }

Her Existence

She is truthful to all eyes she meet
As she is the queen of faith street
Having the look of harmony with the Creator in every
heart beat
She always has the right words for prayer in the house of
God with having a seat
She strives to bring forth the existence of God
As she obeys his law in confirmational nod
She being pure holiness in the dark
She has wisdom to continue life in being scarred among
the holy arch
Joints herself with husband to enlighten the define of
romance
She always has God first before the sexual dance
Decades being as one with another without sin she lives
the meaning of love with God
Her existence gives me passion to live my life thereof
with God.

Sunshine Living

The know of sunshine living is without harm
I cleared my head and said with a will to achieve this everyday
For being in sin harms the soul to be away from Creator
As well the thrill doing wrong hath no worth in any way
I refuse to be sick in depths of wrongdoing
Paradise is a friendly place to be collected in love from Creator
To be in the notion of being good to success the Creator's strong doing
To bliss the whole existence of me in true reality of life
Achieve to be happy in every act with the power of Creator by my side
The wonder to be steady living in positive vibrations
Comes with my will to succeed a life without sin in having nothing to hide
Be a cheer in the darkest moment to all relations

Mysticism

My will to be sunshine living comes from being in the dark, my will to achieve sunshine living will close the dark.

{ **39** }

This Angel

This angel got me going up and down
Thoughts in hurried acts
Creator being amused clown
Feeling with faith having nature reacts
Anyways it has me to flow, I have God to thank in being stable in life's show
Have me pray more, alone has my eyes see the lord to adore
Gives me the will to confess, and anew my path to success
Energize my soul in knowledge, to have faith education higher than college
This angel has me going up and down
Moving around to succeed in the Creator.

This Wednesday
Afternoon

This Wednesday afternoon I thought of you
For I love mom and I have you
Grace of God and his power brings you to life to me,
As though cant enjoy the similar things
We have relation and it sings
Our bond heighten by my love for you in spree
The heated day in the summer is when once you swim me
in the pool
Being the dad , being ever so cool
Knowing the word fun
Without talks of a gun
Water splash memory
Words remember me
Out of your mouth before you know why you said it
Is the exodus of the flashback from your love that lead it
Is the same heat as today in the afternoon of a Wednesday

You been flesh dead for decades now
Our meet is my joy of God being he
The passion to just fleshy bond with you when our meet
is done
Like we use to when I was little being wild and free
And no sin, none
This beautiful powerful sun having the image as that day
at the community pool
Well going inside now to cool.

Shine of Eden

Shine of Eden
Enlighten in the wind
Our king been beaten
To have us better from then
Shine of Eden
Lives in the wind
Our king, symbolically we eaten
His existence showing his glory to where we been
Shine of Eden
Stays in the wind
For our king, we seat in
For our existence is pure innocent from since when
Shine of Eden is in the wind, always near
Shine of Eden is in the wind, always here.